Popular Hits • Level 4

MW00812561

Piano

Arranged by Tom Gerou

This series offers Broadway, pop, and movie music arrangements to be used as supplementary pieces for students. Soon after beginning piano study, students can play attractive versions of favorite classics, as well as the best-known popular music of today.

This book is correlated page-by-page with Lesson Book 4 of *Alfred's Basic Piano Library*; pieces should be assigned based on the instructions in the upper-right corner of the title page of each piece in *Popular Hits*. Since the melodies and rhythms of popular music do not always lend themselves to precise grading, you may find that these pieces are sometimes a little longer and more difficult than the corresponding pages in the Lesson Book. The teacher's judgment is the most important factor in deciding when to assign each arrangement.

When the books in the *Popular Hits* series are assigned in conjunction with the Lesson Books, these appealing pieces reinforce new concepts as they are introduced. In addition, the motivation the music provides could not be better. The emotional satisfaction that students receive from mastering each song increases their enthusiasm to begin the next one.

Printed in USA.

ISBN-10: 1-4706-2739-6
ISBN-13: 978-1-4706-2739-3

Produced by
Alfred Music
P.O. Box 10003
Van Nuys, CA 91410-0003
alfred.com

Cover Photos: Music speakers: © Shutterstock.com / Martin M303 • Headphones: © Shutterstock.com / Jiri Hera

Use with Alfred's Basic Piano Library,
Lesson Book 4, after pages 2–3.

Downton Abbey Theme

(from *Downton Abbey*)

Composed by John Lunn
Arr. by Tom Gerou

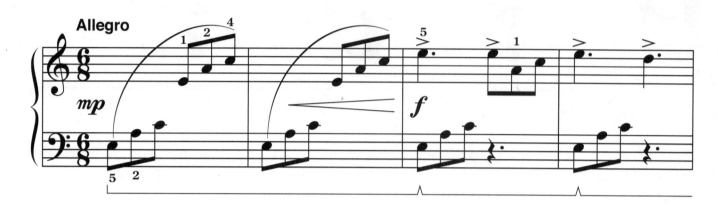

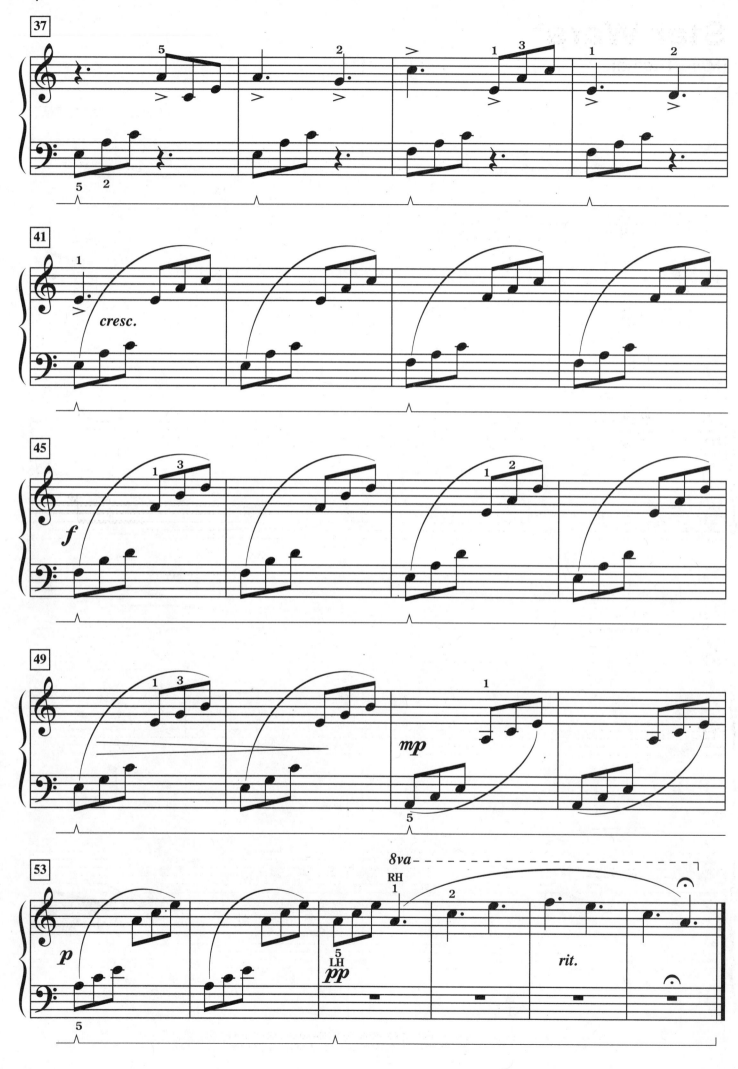

Star Wars®
(Main Theme)

By **JOHN WILLIAMS**

Arr. by Tom Gerou

6

Newt Says Goodbye to Tina

(from *Fantastic Beasts and Where to Find Them*)

Use after pages 8–9.

Composed by James Newton Howard
Arr. by Tom Gerou

Use after page 18.

Firework

Words and Music by
Katy Perry, Mikkel Eriksen, Tor Erik Hermansen,
Sandy Wilhelm and Ester Dean
Arr. by Tom Gerou

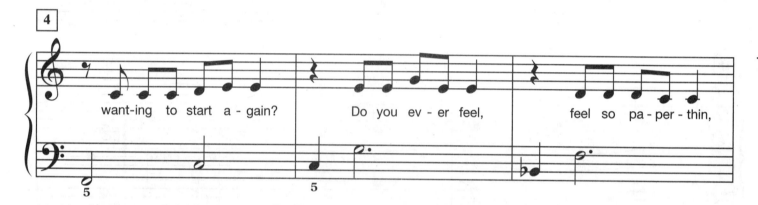

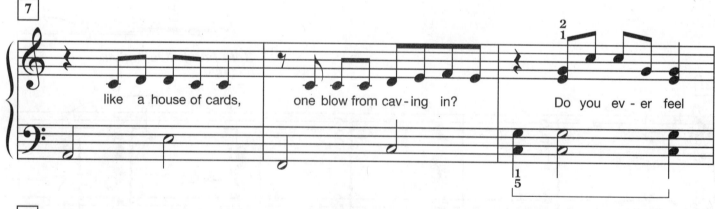

The Magnificent Seven

By Elmer Bernstein
Arr. by Tom Gerou

Moderately bright

14

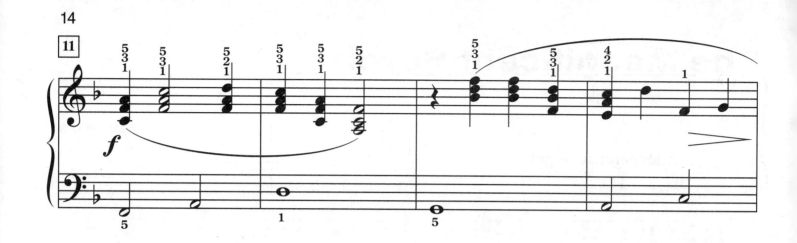

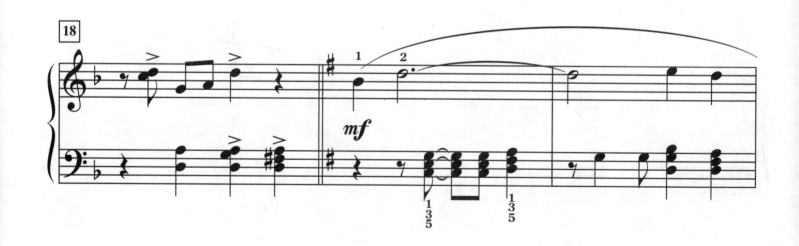

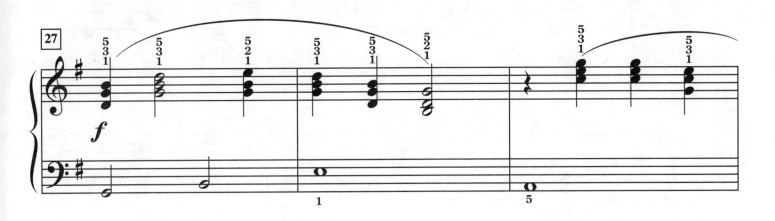

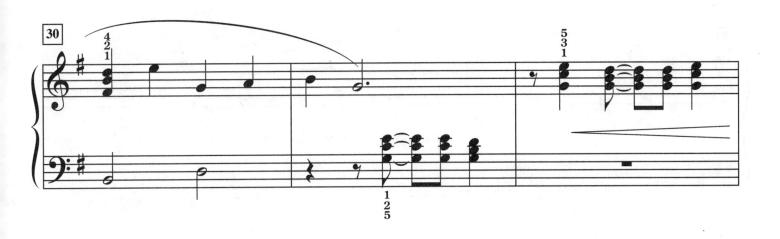

Big Yellow Taxi

Use after pages 20–21.

Words and Music by Joni Mitchell
Arr. by Tom Gerou

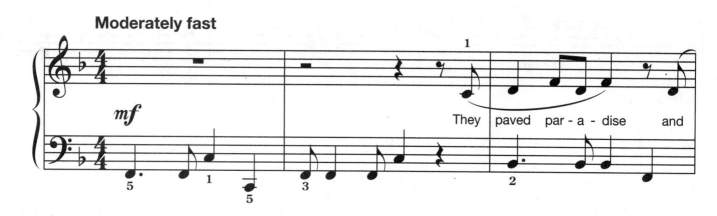

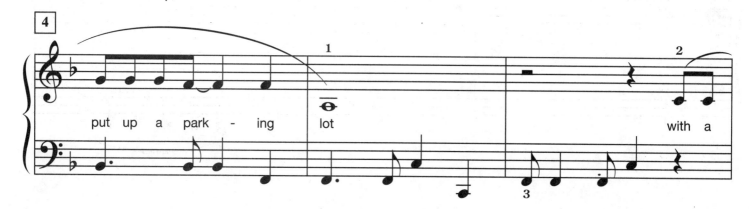

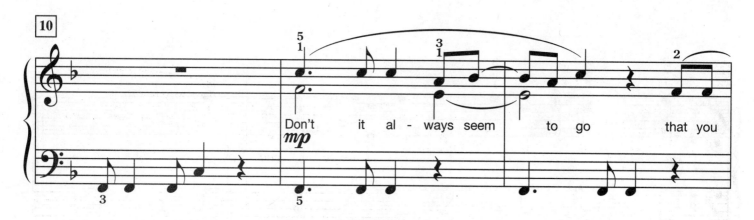

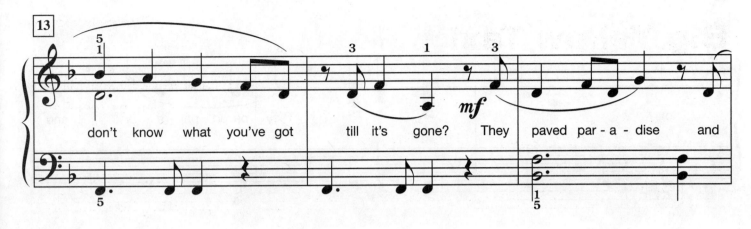

don't know what you've got | till it's gone? They | paved par-a-dise and

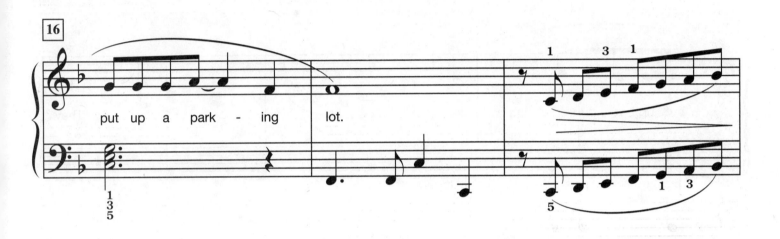

put up a park - ing lot.

Don't it al-ways seem | to go that you | don't know what you've got

till it's gone? They | paved par-a-dise and | put up a park - ing

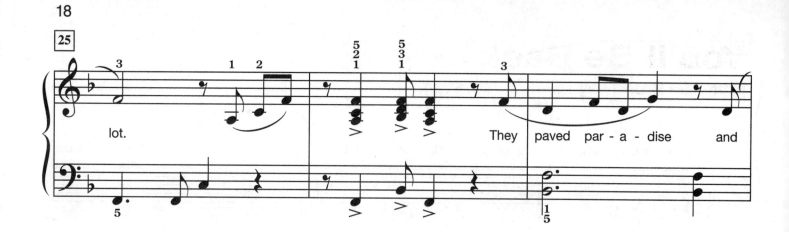

lot.   They paved par - a - dise   and

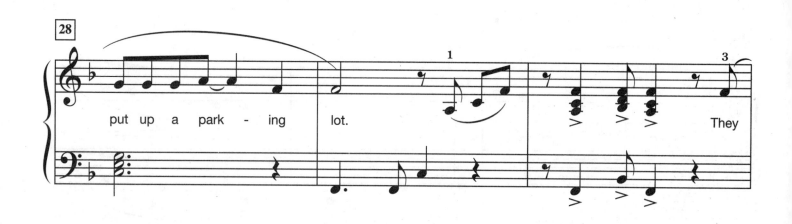

put up a park - ing   lot.   They

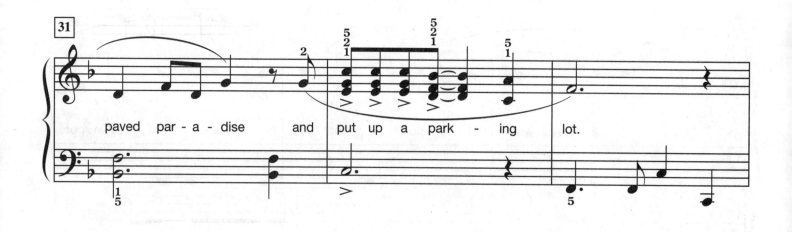

paved par - a - dise   and put up a park - ing   lot.

You'll Be Back
(from the Broadway musical *Hamilton*)

Words and Music by Lin-Manuel Miranda
Arr. by Tom Gerou

Moderate swing tempo

Use after page 25.

Mia & Sebastian's Theme

(from *La La Land*)

By Justin Hurwitz
Arr. by Tom Gerou

Moderately slow, expressively

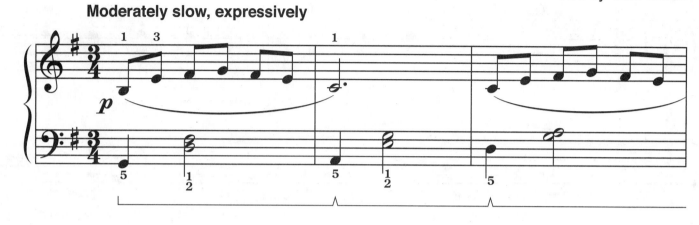

Use after page 31.

Sorry

Words and Music by
Justin Tranter, Julia Michaels, Justin Bieber,
Sonny Moore and Michael Tucker
Arr. by Tom Gerou

Lyrics:

You got-ta go and get an-gry at all of my hon-es-ty,

I know I try but I don't do too well with a-pol-o-gies.

Hope I don't run out of time, can some-one call a ref-er-ee? 'Cause I just

Style

Words and Music by Ali Payami,
Johan Schuster, Max Martin and Taylor Swift
Arr. by Tom Gerou

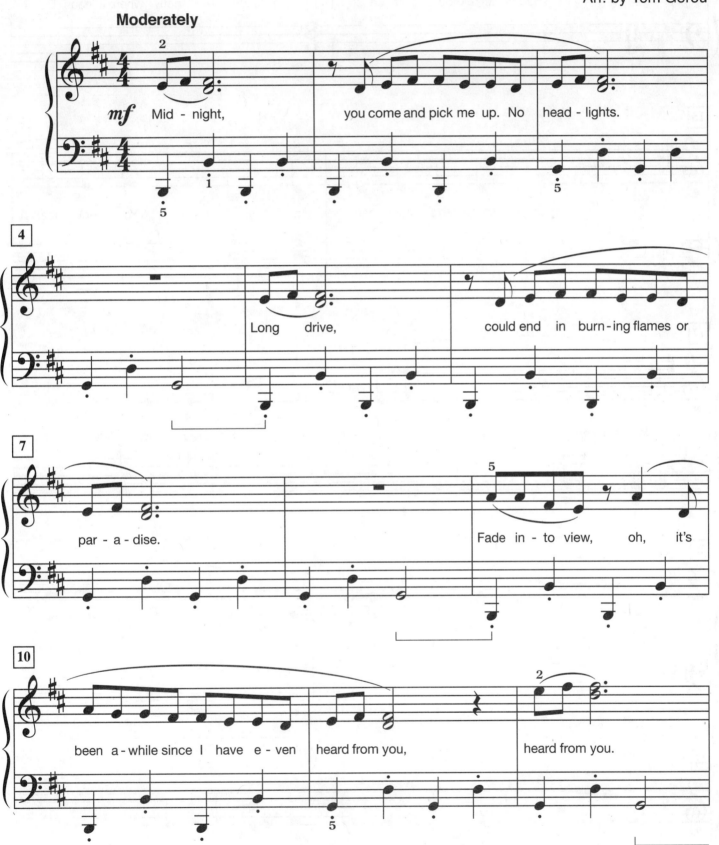

The Pink Panther

Use after pages 34–35.

By Henry Mancini
Arr. by Tom Gerou

Moderato
Both hands 8va lower throughout

Use after page 45.

Jacob's Bakery
(from *Fantastic Beasts and Where to Find Them*)

Composed by James Newton Howard
Arr. by Tom Gerou

Moderate swing tempo

Use after pages 46–47.

How Far I'll Go

(from *Moana*)

Words and Music by Lin-Manuel Miranda
Arr. by Tom Gerou